An Anne Taintor Collection

MJF BOOKS
NEW YORK

Published by MJF Books
Fine Communications
322 Eighth Avenue
New York, NY 10001

I can't be good all *the time*
LC Control Number 2006923170
ISBN-13:   978-1-56731-788-6
ISBN-10:   1-56731-788-X

Designed by Laura Crookston

This edition published by MJF Books in arrangement with Chronicle Books LLC.

Printed in Singapore.

MJF Books and the MJF colophon are trademarks of Fine Creative Media, Inc.

TWP   10   9   8   7   6   5   4   3   2   1

introduction

I haven't always been a bad girl. In grade
school I was considered a goody-two-shoes,
even the nuns thought so. But life does
change one. There were temptations and
opportunities, men and marriages, parties
and mayhem. Eventually, I realized that I
wasn't such a good girl anymore . . . and
that I was having a lot more fun.

I love that my work makes people laugh. I
can't take all the credit, though; everyone
in my family talks exactly like the women
on these pages. I guess it's no surprise that
I found myself carrying on the tradition.

Let's face it, being bad is better. In times
of doubt, may this book remind you that we
can't be good all the time. Besides, who
wants to try?

—Anne Taintor

suddenly she even *felt* cosmopolitan

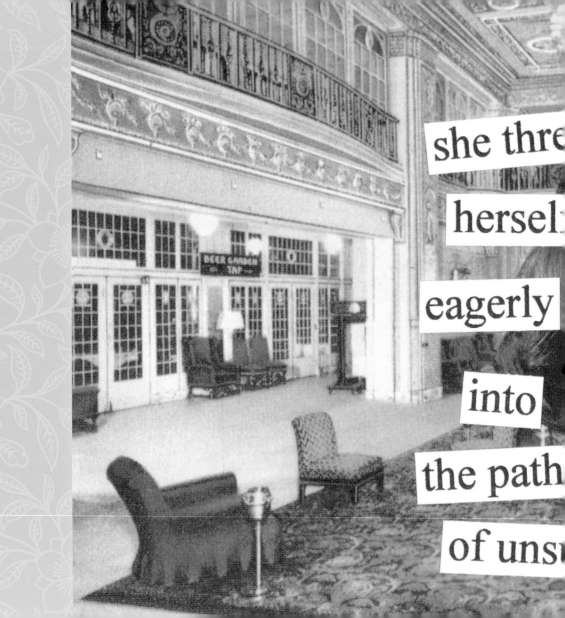

she thre
hersel
eagerly
into
the path
of unsu

he gave
new meaning
to the term
"brut"

she was

eager

to stoop

to his level

born to

be wild

she was tempted

to cause a scene

she had

not yet decided

whether

to use

her power

for good…

or for evil

she was just a little conflicted

maybe *I want* to look cheap

she was determined to buy whatever he was selling

she refused
to let
common sense
cloud her judgement

gee...

she had an opinion

about

everything

he was a blues song
waiting to happen

she was
sure
she
could
make
him
behave

there's such a thing as being *too* emotionally accessible

she liked her men

like her wines...

robust, with a long finish

his story

was thoroughly researched

and delivered

with great dramatic flair

she wasn't sure she *wanted* to live happily ever after

perhaps
it was time
to try
a different corner

they *hated*

to spread

gossip

break a leg, honey

it would,

of course,

have to look

like an accident

was she *ready* for another thrilling episode?

I'm so *happy*

it's

happy hour

let's ignore our mothers' well-meant advice

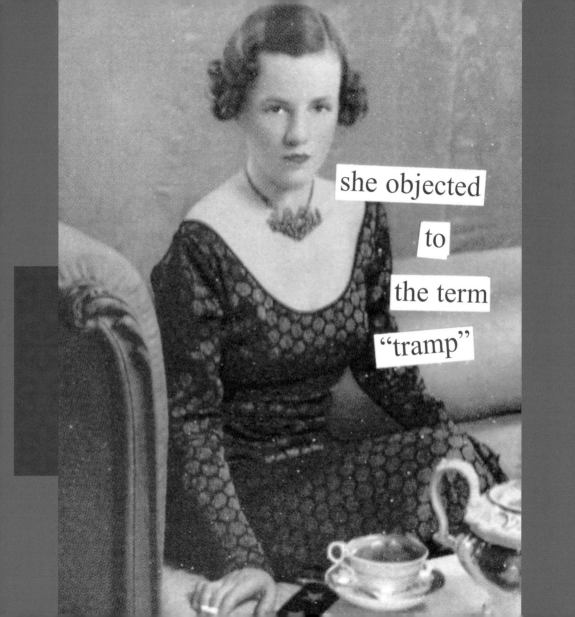

she liked

her men

like her chocolate...

dark and rich

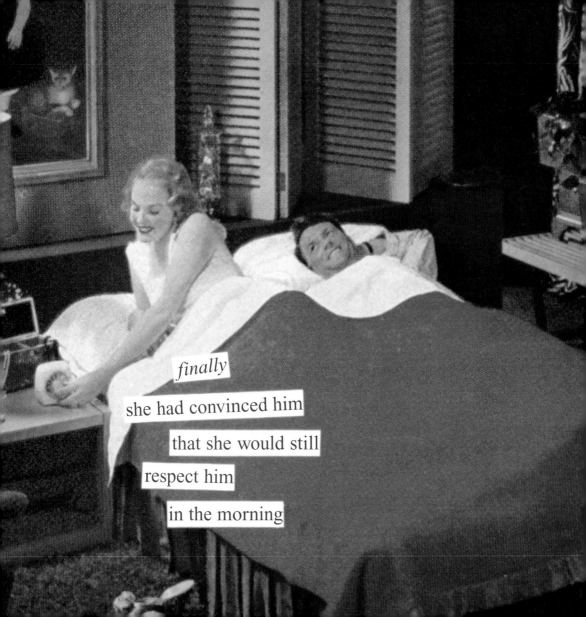

finally

she had convinced him

that she would still

respect him

in the morning

she was

blissfully

unaware

of her peril

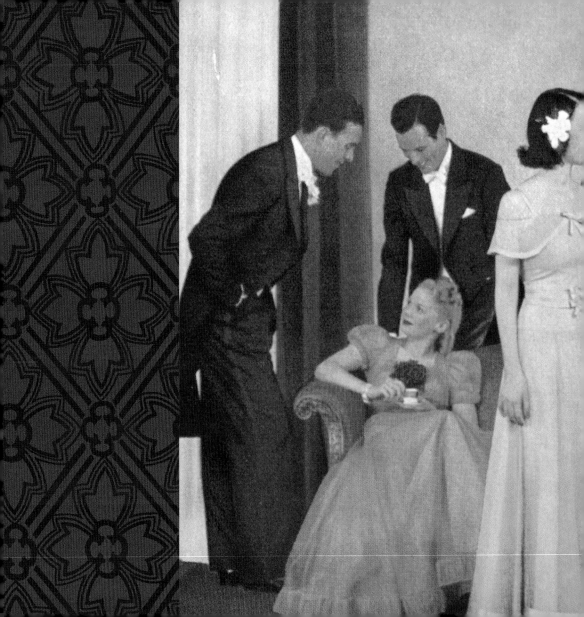

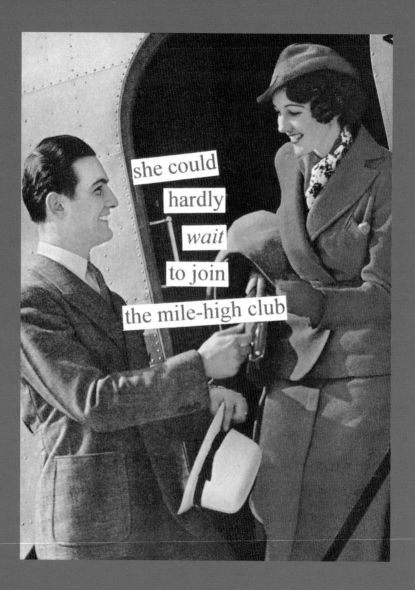

she had
told him
that
she liked to
swing

she thought
of herself
as
a work
in progress

what's
in it
for me?

he couldn't
become
a distant memory
soon enough
to suit her

she was really

quite impressed

by his

breath control

she was over him at last

she could hardly wait to be back in the saddle again

she thought of them as...

a 4H project

she *hated* to think about her sins

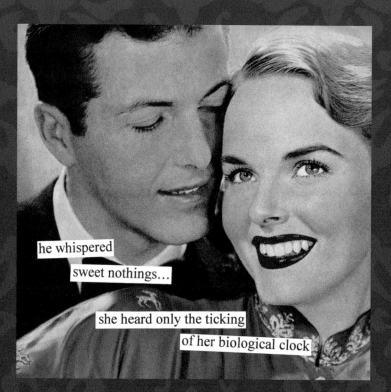

mistakes were made

will I *never* learn?

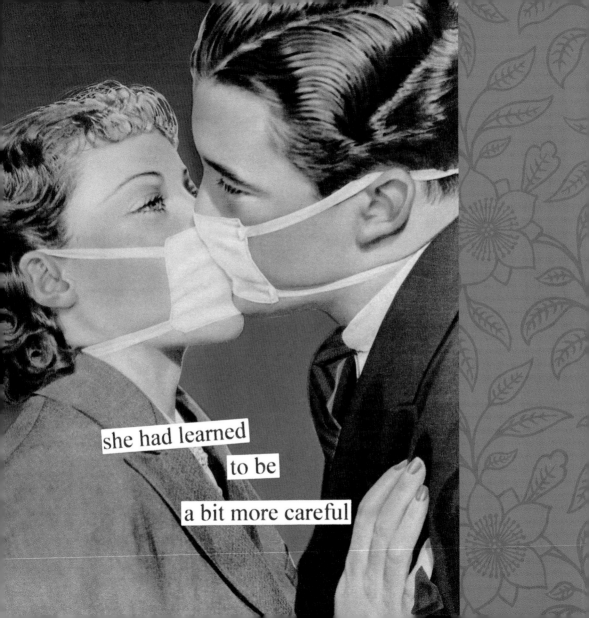

she had learned
to be
a bit more careful

she liked

imaginary

men

best of all

pardon my French

DAYS LIKE THIS
Good Writers on Bad Luck,
Bum Deals & Other Torments

edited by
Samantha Schoech

CBD Publishing